A WINNING SKILLS BOOK

You Can Be Happy!

Joy Berry

Illustrated by Bartholomew

Joy Berry Enterprises

Copyright © Joy Berry, 2022
Originally Published 2013

All rights are reserved.

No part of this book can be duplicated or used without the prior written permission of the copyright owner, except for the use of brief quotations from the book.

For inquiries or permission requests contact the publisher.

Published by Joy Berry Enterprises
www.joyberryenterprises.com

Joy Berry Enterprises

You can be happy if you understand
- what is happiness,
- what makes you happy,
- what you can do to make yourself happy,
- six facts about happiness,
- what you should do when you are unhappy,
- ways to avoid unhappiness, and
- what you should do when you are depressed.

WHAT IS HAPPINESS?

Some people think that happiness is
- fun and
- laughter

However, happiness is not fun and laughter. Sometimes you may experience these things when you are happy, but sometimes you do not. You can be happy without having fun and laughter.

Happiness is a sense of well-being. It is the feeling that you are going to be all right. Happiness is being satisfied. It is being pleased with who you are and what you have. When you are happy you feel glad. You feel joyful.

6 WHAT MAKES YOU HAPPY?

Your mind controls your body.

Your mind also controls your feelings and therefore your happiness.

Step 1: Your mind receives information.

Some of the information it takes is positive. **Positive information** helps to make you happy and thus contributes to your happiness.

Some of the information your mind receives is negative. **Negative information** keeps you from being happy and thus inhibits your happiness.

Step 2: Your mind evaluates whatever information it receives.

It decides whether the information is positive or negative.

Step 3: Your mind decides how you should react to the information it receives.

It determines how you should feel and what you should do about the information it takes in.

Step 4: You react the way your mind tells you to react.

You feel the way your mind tells you to feel, and you do the things your mind tells you to do.

Your feelings and behavior cause you to be happy or sad. Therefore, your happiness is determined by the information your mind receives and by how your mind tells you to react to that information.

WHAT YOU CAN DO TO MAKE YOURSELF HAPPY

You don't have to be unhappy. There are things you can do to make yourself happy.

The first thing you can do to make yourself happy is to **control the information your mind receives.**

Positive information helps to make you happy. Therefore, you should do all you can do to make sure that the information your mind takes in is positive.

Your mind takes in information from outside sources through your fives senses. Whatever you see, hear, touch, taste, and smell becomes the information that your mind processes. Your mind processes all the information it receives. It does not matter where the information originates.

Most information comes into your mind through your eyes and ears.

WHAT YOU CAN DO TO MAKE YOURSELF HAPPY

You should try to control what you **see** and what your **read.**

You will be happier if what you see and read contains positive information.

You should try to control what you **hear**.

You will be happier if what you hear contains positive information.

You can find out if what you are watching, reading, or hearing contains positive information by asking yourself these six questions.

1. Does this information help me appreciate and understand myself and the world around me?
2. Does this information make me want to participate in healthy, worthwhile activities instead of harmful, destructive ones?

3. Does this information teach me worthwhile ideals, values, and beliefs?
4. Does this information show a clear difference between right and wrong? Does it make me want to do what is right?
5. Does this information make clear what is true and what is untrue?
6. Does this information frighten or upset me in any way?

In addition to the information you receive from outside sources, you receive information from the things you say to yourself.

You should try to control the things you say to yourself. You need to make sure that your messages to yourself contain positive information. For example:

- If you tell yourself, "I am going to have a good day," you will most likely have a good day.

You should avoid giving yourself negative information contained in messages such as these:
- I am not good.
- I cannot do anything.
- Nothing good ever happens to me.
- I never get what I want.

You should try to give yourself positive information contained in messages such as these:
- I am a good person.
- I can do many wonderful things.
- Good things can happen to me.
- I have many things for which to be thankful.

The second thing you can do to make yourself happy is to **control the way you react to the information your mind receives.**

Sometimes you cannot control the information your mind takes in. When this happens, you should try to control the way you *react* to the information.

Negative information will not cause unhappiness if you react to it in the right way. To do this, you must keep negative information in perspective. It will help you remember and respond to these six facts:

Fact 1. There are good and bad things about every situation.

Try not to focus on the bad things about a situation. Instead, find the good things and focus your attention on them. This will make you a happier person.

Fact 2. There is something to be gained from every experience.

Experiences that make you feel good may give you pleasure, but experiences that make you feel bad can teach you valuable lessons. Try to learn from the experiences that make you feel bad. This will help you grow and become a better person.

Fact 3. Things could always be worse.

Try to realize that no matter how bad a situation seems to be, it could always be worse. Then, be thankful that it is not worse. Being thankful will help you feel better.

Fact 4. Every problem has a solution.

When you have a problem, try not to waste your time and energy feeling bad about it. Instead realize that your problem has a solution. Then, spend your time and energy finding the solution. This will help you overcome the problems that could keep you from being happy.

Fact 5. "This too shall pass" and "Time heals all wounds."

"This too shall pass" means that as time passes, every experience comes to an end. "Time heals all wounds" means that as time passes, your unhappy experiences are likely to become less painful and you will feel better and better. When you go through an unhappy experience, repeat these sayings to yourself. Remind yourself that at some time the experience will be over and you will feel better again. This can comfort you during your unhappy times.

Fact 6. There is humor in almost every situation.

Try to find something to laugh about when you are sad. Laughing will make you feel better.

The best way to overcome unhappiness is by doing things that make you happy. Find out what makes you feel good. Then do these things when you are unhappy. There are eight activities that usually make people feel good.

Activity 1. Being Kind

Get together with other people. Do nice things for them. They will respond positively to you, and that will make you feel good.

Activity 2. Working

When you work you accomplish something. When you accomplish something, you will feel good.

Activity 3. Playing

Get involved in recreation and activities that are fun. You will feel good if you do something fun.

Activity 4. Laughing

Do something that makes you laugh. Laughing will make you feel good.

Activity 5. Daydreaming

Think about wonderful things. Positive daydreaming is a good way to replace sad thoughts with happy thoughts.

Activity 6. Listening to or Playing Music

Get involved with the kind of music you enjoy. Listen to it, sing it, dance to it. Music can make you feel good.

Activity 7. Appreciating or Creating Beauty

Surround yourself with natural or man-made beauty. Make something beautiful yourself. Beautiful things can also make your feel good.

Activity 8. Paying Attention to Your Physical Appearance

Do something to improve your physical appearance. Clean yourself up, dress up, or do something positive to change the way you look. When you look good, you will feel good.

There are four things you can do to avoid unhappiness.

1. Keep your body healthy.

It is difficult to be happy when your body is sick. It is important to eat good food, get plenty of exercise and rest, and do whatever else is necessary to keep your body healthy.

2. Create happy surroundings.

As often as possible, surround yourself with people you enjoy being around.

Also, try to be in places that make you happy. If you are in a place that makes you sad, do whatever you can to change it. You may need to organize, clean, or redecorate the area.

3. Make happiness a habit.

A habit is something you do so often for so long that you do it without thinking.

Make a list of the things you enjoy doing, and make sure you do at least one every day.

4. Have happy thoughts.

Start and end every day with happy thoughts. Think about the good things that have happened, and think about the good things that are about to happen.

Let your thoughts lead the way and your happiness will follow.

If everything you have done to maintain your happiness doesn't work, you might be depressed.

If you are continually depressed you are experiencing *chronic depression.*

If you continually encounter alternate feelings of intense elation and extreme depression, you are experiencing **manic depression.**

Both chronic and manic depressions are disorders that require professional help to resolve. A psychiatrist (a medical doctor who specializes in mental, emotional, or behavioral disorders) is the best resource for helping with depression.

To help patients overcome depression, psychiatrists often recommend one or more of the following:
- lifestyle changes,
- prescriptive diets,
- vitamin therapy,
- talk therapy, and/or
- prescriptive medications (anti-depressants).

CONCLUSION

You can **be happy** if you want to be happy and you are willing to do what you need to do to make yourself happy.

www.ingramcontent.com/pod-product-compliance
Lightning Source LLC
Chambersburg PA
CBHW081408070526
44583CB00020B/2726